The Book of HATE

Copyright Lance Hodge, 2016
All rights reserved

ISBN-13: 978-1534765450

Printed in the United States of America

Updated: 7/19

Note: It's not *all* your fault, if you've been wearing those rose-colored glasses, or if you've fallen victim to political and media manipulation; they've been good at it. It's infected many of us, nearly half of us it seems, and it started long ago, in our schools, with all those liberal ~~teachers~~ indoctrinators.

So take a moment to remove those glasses, to see with *your* eyes, to hear with *your* ears, and to push aside, if just for a few dozen pages, what you've been *told* to see and hear.

We all have common sense but sometimes it can be clouded, sometimes those who would use us for some nefarious plans can do so without us realizing it, but *they* realize *exactly* what they're doing, and their goal *is* indoctrination, not critical thought.

But we can cut the strings of the puppeteer and walk free, and in the end, we can see those who seek to *control* us and to transform America into some *other* country for what they are, *evil*.

Lance Hodge

"Liberals claim to want to give a hearing to other views, but then are shocked and offended to discover that there *are* other views."

William F. Buckley Jr.

Contents

The Book

Of

HATE

By Lance Hodge

This book is a bit of a hodge-podge, a compilation of several different approaches to this subject. This isn't about 'me' or any person, it's about stereotypes, generalizations, purposeful misdirection, and outright lies. It's the FOX News vs. CNN syndrome, and what your world view may come to be if you listen to too much of either one.

The media is NOT our friend, the media, on the right and left, has an agenda. Both speak of fairness in reporting, and fairness is, as far as the media is concerned, a matter of what supports their agenda, and tends to prop up their and their viewer's world view of things. And so the "News" should be taken with a big grain of salt, it is at its core bent on shaping the world into their view of it, by shaping the perceptions of voters, and, they do a good job, especially with liberals, who seem easy to shape. The "news" is really a political animal, **truth** is not the goal, it is often a problem to be overcome.

My job here is to shed some light on a few things, mostly upon the supposedly monolithic, and distorted, world view held by conservatives. I'm using myself as an example here but these principles apply to most of us conservatives.

I hope to set some things straight, but things like this, **opinions** about things, are easily misunderstood. Let's see if we can understand some of these opinions a little better.

P.S.
We need to start with the premise that sometimes someone is wrong, and someone is right, and sometimes it's just a matter of personal preference, not necessarily right or wrong. But, and this is important, sometimes, yes, sometimes, someone IS **right**, and someone IS **wrong**. That's important to remember! Especially if YOU are wrong.

<u>Note to liberals</u>: At the outset here, in hopes that you've gotten at least this far in your reading, some food for thought:

Hypocrisy. Liberals just can't seem to recognize this in themselves. You ought to have some <u>core values</u> that guide you, but…

In our recent history, if a democratic President gets involved in a war, you don't hear much outcry; a republican gets involved in a war, and all the liberal media starts a daily body count, and a constant reminder that the war is unjust, expensive, racist, etc.

Democrat healthcare plan, wonderful. Republican healthcare plan; they hate women, minorities, the elderly, and want all people dead.

Spending. Democrat debt, no problem. Republican debt; unpatriotic, stealing from our grandchildren.

Etc.

Chapter One

HATE

Hate. That's a strong word. That word is used freely against many of us with **opinions**, *diverse* opinions. Of course *diverse* means *different*, and you may not know this but diverse is BAD in liberal circles, if your *diverse* opinion is *different* from the opinion of those who hold another opinion, since *diversity*, it seems, really means, *"You must think the way I think."* Diversity, *difference*, only works, by *liberal* standards, when we are the SAME. For as much as they (liberals) tout *diversity*, they don't believe it. Look at the rancor and violence when liberals *protest* and you'll see how inclusive of diverse views they are, *they aren't*.

Note: The liberal reading this, if any liberal would, is done about now, that first paragraph was too much, too much HATE. They won't listen to the opposing view. Conservatives DO listen to the opposing view, and find it CRAZY, for the most part. Conservatives find the liberal argument wrong because their arguments commonly fly in the face of FACTS. The liberal will find the conservative argument wrong because, it hurts their feelings, or is somehow 'hateful.' **Facts** *should matter. And, if I didn't lose the liberals with that first paragraph, I lost them with this one; they DON'T WANT TO HEAR THE TRUTH.*

Note #2: How does a liberal come to the conclusions they come to? Not facts, so, it's the rantings of their peer group, the talking heads on some liberal media, some liberal teacher, or it seems to *be the 'trend' on their social media, but it's not **facts**. I recently tried to reason with my liberal daughter. She says the prisons are full of black and brown people because of a white racist judicial system, and of course racist police officers, and of course a racist white majority society. And when I presented her with the FACT that most crime is committed by black and brown people, well, her excuse changed to 'why' they did it; because they were poor, they had gangs in their neighborhood, and somehow whitey made them do it. Do you care 'why' the criminal rapes, robs, or murders? I don't, at least not when it comes to putting them in jail or not. Are you just destined to be a criminal if you grow up in a bad environment, or is it a choice? I'll help you here, IT'S A CHOICE. Is the judge supposed to say, "Well, you robbed that liquor store and killed the owner, but, since your mom is a drug addict and your father left when you were two, and your brother is in a gang, and your family is on welfare, well, it's not your fault. Have a nice day, case dismissed." Facts just don't matter to liberals. The liberal's 'core values' are fluid, they'll change as the media opinion changes, they are based on **emotion** not fact.*

Somebody's got something wrong here, sometimes, on some things, we can't always *compromise*. Sometimes something **is** black and white, like this is black, ●, and this is white, □. Sometimes, the *facts* are *facts*, and we can't wish them away; and for some, that's hard to take. Those "facts" become "hateful."

The idea of this book is to help some of you (liberals) understand 'the other side.' Too many people are easily influenced, too many are quick to *follow*, too many don't seek to *really* understand an issue, they simply move with the flow of opinion, they become lemmings marching in line with their peer group and the opinions of their chosen media source. As you read on you'll see the whole point here is to help *liberals* see the light, to realize that what they've been fed regarding *conservatives* is wrong. And of course, liberals will welcome this, they'll be happy to be set straight, right? *(For you liberals, who I hope are still reading, this is a short book, you should bite the bullet and keep reading.)*

First, before we go any further, I'll point out a simple truth, something I **do** understand at the outset, a truth that makes a book like this, well, *useless*. Generally, you can't get a liberal to even *read* something like this, and it's written for *them*, so, again, useless, a waste of time, preaching to the choir. But, I'm writing it anyway, mainly because of my daughters, who also won't care.

My two daughters are liberals, *hopeless* liberals most likely, but I'm hoping they will sit down and read this, not that I expect it to 'change them' but, *wishing* it would.

And I'm hoping this explanation of what we conservatives think, when shared by other conservatives with their friends and family, will hit home to some of *your* liberal family and acquaintances, but, I'm not holding my breath.

My daughter says she's embarrassed by the things I post on Facebook; the *facts* really bother liberals. Liberals also seem overly concerned with what their friends might think if they were to read some dissenting view on their social media. How about reminding those friends that people can, and do, have *other* opinions, and that it's smart to listen to those other views, because, you might just find out that you've got it wrong! For example, "I" listen to liberals and their views, a LOT, that's how I know that most of those views are so CRAZY, and based on *emotion* not fact. I don't mind hearing such views, it gives me a chance to comment on why they are so wrong. Gee, that's 'embarrassing' or 'rude' or 'trolling' to have another point of view, or, is it the essence of our life here on this little planet, interacting with each other and from time to time trying to convince other people that they've got something wrong, especially when that 'wrong' view is *dangerous*. Liberal viewpoints are *often* dangerous, not only to our collective well-being, but to the fabric of this Nation.

I was listening to the radio a few minutes ago, (this was during the 2016 election cycle) and a caller to a radio station said she supported Hillary Clinton, and the host asked her to give just *one* reason why, and the caller said, *"Because she's honest."* To a conservative that's the mating call of a lemming, it squeals and screeches in our head because it announces the liberal as someone who just CAN'T hear or see, or *think*, apparently. But to the liberal, when hearing a statement like that, they don't even blink.

Note: Since this was first written we have had an incredible event, Donald Trump was elected President. Hello liberals! It seems that half of the country was on the WRONG side of American values and beliefs; that would be the *liberal side*. You'd think you might want to pay attention to that election, and that other half of our Country, you just might be wrong about some of your "core beliefs."

Note: Even though they did it right this time, I don't trust voters to "get it right." Barack Obama proved that point twice, but there is a difference here, it's what the candidates *stood for*. One, *American values*, and America first, the other, a liberal globalist view, in which America comes second. One of those views is "right" and one is *so* "wrong."

Conservatives and Liberals see things VERY differently. Just take a few topics, listed below, and you can see that such things are *very* divisive, and that Conservatives and Liberals tend to have strong, and opposing, opinions about such things:

The border, guns, war, the criminal justice system, racism, sexism, LGBTQ issues, capitalism, socialism, race, abortion, oil, global warming, healthcare, welfare, "free" school, the minimum wage, 'The War on Women' and the list goes on.

Conservatives and Liberals, Republicans and Democrats; they see the world quite differently, often the difference is night and day. It's a matter of the media you listen to, the opinions held by your peers, and perhaps some *defect* in the liberal brain. *(Sorry, not trying to insult, but the prefrontal cortex problem (defect) in liberals is real, we'll touch on that later.)*

It would be wise to try to better understand each other, if possible, and this is my attempt, as a conservative, to help you liberals better understand what you have so misunderstood for so long. You, liberals, have been falling hook-line-and sinker for the liberal media's hogwash about conservatives, and I'm here to help you pull that hook out, all while realizing you LIKE that hook. Here goes.

Do you remember the *Chic-fil-a* controversy? It's come back from time to time since its original appearance, but it got a lot of attention at the time. The founder of *Chic-fil-a* (a fast food chicken sandwich place) was very religious, and he let it be known during the whole gay marriage controversy, that he believed marriage should be between *one man and one woman* (I know, a CRAZY idea.) This had *nothing* to do with his *Chic-fil-a* restaurants, it was just *his opinion*, but a whole boycott of *Chic-fil-a* was organized, and it included a desire to run he and his chicken sandwich restaurants out of business. The whole thing backfired and *Chic-fil-a* became more popular than ever, but that's beside the point. The founder of *Chic-fil-a* was considered a *hater* for his *personal views* about marriage, and according to the pro-gay LGBTQ liberals, his business should be closed down. The employees at *Chic-fil-a* were free to marry whoever they wanted, it was just the owner's *personal* views on marriage that were so despised that his very livelihood should be destroyed. **Diversity**. So someone like that *Chic-fil-a* founder was a *hater*, simply because his *opinion* differed from that of others. You liberals don't see a problem there? Maybe you ought to look up the word "Diversity" then try looking up "Tolerance."

Some of us will be OK with people marrying whoever, or, perhaps, *whatever*, but some of us will see this differently. For those who believe in The Bible as the inspired word of God, well, they think they have it on high authority that marriage must be between one man and one woman. *I'm not religious*, but I see this issue in the light of the history of society, in the United States and also around the world. This concept of marriage as a sacred union between one man and one woman is pretty universal, with notable exceptions, but generally a universal *norm* for civilized peoples. Oh, and until just a few years ago, Hillary Clinton and Barack Obama were all on board with the *one man one woman* definition of marriage, until it served them, politically, to change that position. Did you liberals know that about Hillary and Barack? Don't you see how liberals are playing all of us? A liberal's views of right and wrong tend to sway in the wind, and change according to the current political climate.

I'm not real keen on changing things that have been the norm for eons to suit the current trend of the last few years, that seems a bit rash. That's the general *conservative* view, to see things in terms of *norms*, and to be reluctant to toss out those norms without some serious consideration. Again, we have diversity of opinion, which is also the norm, we won't always agree, that's what *diversity* is all about.

As of the writing of this book the whole transgender bathroom issue is BIG news. As with views on marriage, and views on nearly every topic, there are some who have differing opinions on *this* subject (Oh the humanity!) Some believe you *are* whatever gender you *feel like*. Caitlyn Jenner is a *woman*, apparently, because she *feels* like one. I guess it helps that she dresses like one, tries to act like one, takes female hormone injections, had saline water bags implanted into 'her' chest to look like boobs, and has now had her penis removed and a vagina made. And Chaz Bono is a *man*, because he *feels* like one, dresses like one, tries to act like one, takes male hormone injections, has had his boobs cut off and, well I have no idea if 'he' has had a penis made or not. But to many, especially young people, these people, and many like them, have *become* another gender.

<u>Note</u>: Jenner and Bono still have the *wrong* DNA floating around in their bodies, they haven't figured out how to get rid of *that* yet.

Some people say they should be able to change their driver's licenses to say *Male* or *Female* as they *choose*, and should even be able to change their *birth certificates*, to reflect their 'new' gender. They say gender can be, wrongly, 'assigned' at birth and can, on a whim, be *reassigned* to something else. Fine. So, some people have THAT view. Others, well some people think that no matter what parts you get cut off or surgically created, or how hormone injections change your body hair or bone structure or skin, or how you dress and act, well, if you were born a male you'll always *really* be a male, and girls will always *be* girls. I know, CRAZY. And, apparently, in this world where diversity is championed, we just can't have these *diverse* views, somebody is *right*, and somebody is *wrong*, and those who think male means male and female means female, well, they are SO wrong, they are such HATERS. The transgender community will consider you transphobic and a *hater* until *you believe what they believe*. The views on this subject are more often than not harshly divided, with little wiggle room to compromise.

Here's my take. I know it's CRAZY but I think you *can't really* change your *actual* sex. I think it really is (and this is transgender nitroglycerin) it really IS a man dressing up like a woman or a woman dressing up like a man. I'm taking how they 'feel' out of this. Facts are facts. Men can't *become* women, and women can't *become* men. They can't. That's not an opinion, that's a biologic fact. Really. It is. A *fact*. I know, science is so *hateful*. But, and this is important, to me at least, I totally accept this transgender thing as a *real* thing. I know that they do 'feel' like the other gender. Fine. And me, well I'm ok with them using the bathroom that fits that *feeling* **and** their new appearance. Fine. I don't care. And here's the rub. There's a *problem* with the transgender community, they don't just want to use the bathroom that matches their feelings and appearance, they've BEEN doing that with no problem for decades, they want a LAW that blurs the gender line, and, when we go down that road, well, *Houston, we've got a problem.*

Some guys are weirdos, perverts, and predators, and this is mostly a 'guy' thing. Make a law that says you can use whatever bathroom, changing room, *shower*, etc., that you *feel* like, and those weirdos, perverts, and predators will take advantage of it. BAD THINGS WILL HAPPEN, guaranteed, to grown women, to teenagers, and to little children, bad things will happen *because of such laws*, that's a fact, don't even try to doubt it (it's already been happening.) So, me, I'm against such *laws*, because of the unintended consequences, not because of Caitlyn Jenner or Chaz Bono, or people like them. I know, I'm a transphobic transgender hater, just ask Bruce Springsteen. But, am I really? No, I'm not, *I don't care*. And this is generally the conservative stance on this, it's Donald Trump's stance. Conservatives don't necessarily *approve* of it, but they are *tolerant* of it. People can do what they want as far as such gender issues, in my world, and in most of the conservative world, but, do I think it's *normal*, nope. Maybe someday it will be, but right now, with WAY less than 1% of our population transgender, it's NOT *normal*. That right there is very offensive to the transgender community, since *normal* is what they are striving for, that and a redefinition of what *gender* means, and a change in the scientific method apparently, to redefine what male and female means. The whole chromosome thing is very offensive to the trans community. *Chromosomes are such haters!* If Chaz Bono comes in the restroom while I'm in there, I don't give a shit (bad use of words here) but, I don't care, why would I? And, truth be told here, especially to all you hardcore bathroom Nazis on the right, it would be really *weird* to force 'her' into the ladies room, *really* weird, and, nobody is doing that, it's *not* a problem, this entire controversy is a solution looking for a problem, not the other way around.

Just a quick reality check here. If you got a **male** cat or dog, but the cat or dog really *wanted* to be a *female* cat or dog, and you got it a 'girl' cat or dog lease and collar, and maybe a nice girl cat or dog outfit; is your male cat or dog now a female cat or dog? Is it? Did you say "yes" it is *now a female*? If you did… ok, you are REALLY a liberal, congratulations! P.S. Ask your vet this question. I know, veterinarians can be such haters.

In the news recently, a trans 'girl' just beat all the other actual girls in a track meet, is that fair? I say no. A transgender 'female' MMA fighter beat the hell out of an *actual* woman fighter, breaking her face bones etc., is that fair, is gender really fluid? I say no.

Note: There *are* differences between men and women, and male and female, even cats and dogs! You can look that up, it's true. There's a move now to include women in the military draft. It MUST happen if there's no difference between genders, it's only *fair*. Are you liberal women ready for that? If we need more soldiers and there aren't enough volunteers, or if some big war breaks out, they'll give you a gun and you'll have to go kill people; is THAT ok with the liberal left, apparently.

The trans community would tell you they are so oppressed, and this bathroom stuff is just one example of that, it's the new civil rights movement, the transgender issue is just like skin color. Really? Have people, and the government, been keeping Jenner and Bono out of the restroom they want to go into? I don't think so. It's the trans communities' agenda to *normalize* all this and to insist that gender is *fluid*. They insist that there is only how we *feel*, and that's what counts, and they need YOU to believe what *they* believe, or, you are full of HATE.

16

So yes, we have people all worked up on both sides of this bathroom thing, and it's because the trans community wants to put this into LAW. They want to redefine the most basic of human existence, that of our gender. They want the LAW changed, which, as we've already discussed, opens the door to some real harm from the weirdos, perverts, and predators. Is that point of view so hard to embrace? That such laws WILL harm women. I'm a *man*, I spell M-A-N (song reference) and I'll admit it, men as a group have a LOT more weirdos, perverts, and predators on *their* team. I've got an idea for now, women who've *become* men, or at least look a LOT like men, and would fool most men, like Chaz Bono, fine, they can use the men's room, *legally*, fine, put *that* into law. But let's leave the *men in the women's room thing* ambiguous for a while, maybe 10,000 years, until men evolve a bit more.

There's a reason for the title of this book. A couple of years ago "Hate" was the thing, conservatives were *haters*. It didn't take long for that to be replaced by "racist." No matter how I explain this stuff, or how others might, if our opinion is different from *their* opinion, well, we're *haters*, or now, *racists*. Example: I can tell you I don't care what color Barack Obama's skin is, and that's the truth, I don't care, but if I don't like him, well, I'm a *racist*. That's what liberals do, *facts* just don't seem to matter, it is *emotion* that wins the day (again, the defective prefrontal cortex, which we'll talk about later.)

Why do we, conservatives, have to HATE so much? Liberals have been trying, and successfully, to redefine a *difference of opinion* as 'hate.' As you might be able to tell already, these different opinions we've been talking about here are *not* hateful, they're just *different opinions*.

Another hateful example: I HATE Mexicans and Black people, apparently. The facts do get in the way, a lot. *"The jails are full of black and brown people."* Because of our racist legal system, of course. Or, black and brown people do most of the crimes. There are LOTS of statistics, and I could list them… but if you're inclined toward the "Black lives matter" side, well, facts won't matter to you. And, if you can accept the *facts*, well, you probably understood all this 'racist criminal justice system' stuff was just that, *racist BS*, from a race obsessed *liberal and black community*. When most crime is committed by black and brown people, well, there'll be more black and brown people in jail and prison, duh. You don't need racist whites or *white privilege* to explain this, you just need to understand who is doing most of the crime! Duh.

If I became a liberal...

To become a liberal, I'd have to think massive illegal immigration is a good thing. I'd have to welcome waves of immigrants from all over the world to flood into our country, even those that hate us, even those who would destroy our country. I'd have to believe that Islam does not seek global domination, that it can coexist peacefully with other religions, that their doctrines do not subjugate and demean women, that they do not hate and abuse dogs (a little divergent, but a vast number of Muslims hate dogs, and beat them, and torture them, did you know that?) I'd have to believe that a majority Muslim country would at least tolerate LGBTQ rights, even their right to exist. I'd have to believe that no country should have border walls, that a massive welfare state is preferable to a nation that limits such welfare and seeks to move everyone up and out of poverty by encouraging self-reliance and hard work. I'd have to think that guns are evil, and people have no right to self-defense. I'd have to rethink my views on race, and start judging people on the color of their skin, not upon their character and their actions. I would need to accept the view that shouting down an opposing opinion is a good thing, stopping the free flow of ideas is preferable to free speech, and that any speech that presents an opposing view is hate speech, or fascism, or whatever, but that it should be shut down. I'd have to think that to protest means it's ok to burn things and destroy property, and to be physically violent to others. I'd have to embrace a dishonest media, and dismiss facts in favor of emotion. All this, makes it unlikely I could ever become a liberal. I'm a conservative, and that's ok with me.

Chapter Two

"Reports of my death are greatly exaggerated"

"I do not fear death. I had been dead for billions and billions of years before I was born, and had not suffered the slightest inconvenience from it."
Mark Twain

"Each night, when I go to sleep, I die.
And the next morning, when I wake up, I am reborn."
Mahatma Gandhi

"No one really knows why they are alive until they know what they'd die for."
Martin Luther King Jr.

"When writers die they become books, which is, after all, not too bad an incarnation."
Jorge Luis Borges

~

Special thanks to Mark Twain, who in May of 1897 wrote this note… which is often misquoted.

James Ross Clemens, a cousin of mine was seriously ill two or three weeks ago in London, but ~~[crossed out]~~ ~~[crossed out]~~ is well now. ~~[crossed out]~~ ~~[crossed out]~~ The report of my illness grew out of his illness, the report of my death was an exaggeration.

Mark Twain

This book is born of misunderstanding. We misunderstand *hate*, we misunderstand and mislabel *racism*, *bigotry*, and *homophobia*, we misunderstand a LOT of other things. We are very polarized, and usually because of false narratives created by a divisive media with an *agenda*. Most of us are misunderstood at one time or another, and some of us are *never* fully understood. We also die. It is a shame when both of these things collide.

One of those quotes at the beginning of this Chapter, this one *"When writers die they become books, which is, after all, not too bad an incarnation."* That is perhaps the reason for this book, most of us don't want to be misunderstood, and for my immediate friends and family this should set the facts straight. When I die I will become this book, sort of, and at least I've set 'my' record straight, and for others like me who might be misunderstood or misrepresented, I may be speaking for you as well.

A few days ago, I died. For all intents and purposes, to some, I had gone to the great beyond. Like Twain, it was "Greatly exaggerated" a mix up, a misunderstanding, a rumor, a mistake. Someone with the same first name, who worked in the same town, and our occupations although different revolved in the same circles, well, he died, and someone thought he was me, and that person told somebody who told somebody who posted something online and, well, I got a few emails.

"I hope this isn't true but I heard you were dead, are you?" Or something to that effect. A former co-worker, a few former students, all sending a final note into the ether to someone who may or may not be alive. I wrote them back, telling them I was *not* dead, which was a very empowering thing to be able to announce, perhaps we should all try it from time to time, especially when things are rough… "I'm not dead, yet!"

This little event brought a few things home to me. A reminder, although I didn't need this one, that we are all dying, especially those of us who now qualify for senior discounts. And another reminder, and this is the one that particularly annoyed me, that we might die being misunderstood, misclassified, misrepresented.

In light of a recent political tsunami, namely Donald Trump, I was especially sensitive to *political* misrepresentations, having witnessed them daily in the various media about various political figures, and the ones that bothered me most were those that misrepresented what *I* believed, simply because I, reluctantly, belonged to a particular political party. This political gamesmanship is the regular routine, but it is disheartening how many people are easily led, how carelessly and purposely the media lies, how easily and unresistingly those who are lied to *accept* the lies, and how some of these people who march in line with the other lemmings, and who happily don their rose-colored glasses on so many issues, are my friends and family.

I'll simply set some things straight, for me, and for many of we (conservatives) who are misunderstood, or who are lumped into some group or another, and who may not deserve to be in that group.

Now you don't have to believe this, as a matter of fact if you are on the opposing side of the political spectrum you *won't* believe this, but, it's true. We all know there are exceptions to the rule, but there *are* rules, or in this case *generalities* that are *generally*, and in this case, true. So here we go. My attempt to set things straight, in case I do die one day. I don't want anyone saying or thinking something about me because someone in the 'media' led them to believe that people like *this* believe *that*. *(Remember, this isn't about 'me' per say, few people know me or care about what I think, but this whole misrepresentation thing is largely universal, if you listen to the media you know that.)* The media, in case you haven't noticed, and millions of us haven't, are *not* our friends. The media, for the most part, is a political apparatus of the liberal end of the political spectrum. Duh. Oh, that's right, millions of you don't know this. Sorry. Here we go, a brief run-down of me, who is *typical*, except for one atypical 'belief' or non-belief that I'll get to later, well, maybe two, but mostly typical… and, for you other 'Conservatives' or 'Republicans' well, if you identify with my plight here you might want to send this book to *your* friends and family, to set things straight. Truth-be-told nobody cares what "I" think, or probably what 'you' think, but we all like to be *understood*, or at least, not *misunderstood*. So this is more a general manifesto about **Conservatives vs. Liberals**, not so much some particular *person's* beliefs.

My sister often introduces me to people like this *"This is my brother, he's a Republican."* These introductions are most often to her liberal friends, which is really like saying *"This is my brother, he's mentally ill, make sure you don't like him."* She probably doesn't think of the negative impact of what she's doing but she should, it's rude. I wouldn't think of introducing her to my conservative friends as *"This is my sister, she's an enemy to this Country and to our Constitution, you should hate her."*

I'm a mostly *typical* Republican. I vomited just a little in my mouth when I wrote that. For at least a decade now, longer really, that moniker, *Republican*, is a real tough label to stick on my shirt, but, I'm a Republican. *Conservative*, is a MUCH better label. But we don't have that party, we haven't had any *viable* party other than Democrat or Republican in my lifetime, and before, and I'm oldish. In recent years we've had "Tea Party" as a pseudo-party, representing the more 'right-wing' wing of the Republican party, or as the Democrats would say, the crazed Bible-thumping, gun-toting, racist, homophobe, anti-abortion, women-hating, backward, hick, nearly retarded faction of mentally ill barely literate Conservatives. Truth be told, and that's what I'm doing here, I identify with *Tea Party* principles, not Republican 'principles' (Do *they* have some?)

Note to those who don't like people repeating themselves. I had written Chapter Two a while back, and then I wrote Chapter One, and, being dyslexic apparently, I added Chapter Two after Chapter One and then realized I'd repeated myself a bit. As you'll most likely notice, I'm just *writing* this, no outline, no real plan, just writing, and thinking, so if this is somewhat disjointed, or a bit rambley, (apparently not an actual word) or, when I repeat myself a bit, well, I know, but that's how I put this little rant together, and some things bear repeating, so here goes…

Republicans are racists. First, I'm not going to offer up 'proof' of all these assertions, you could look this stuff up, but there would be other sources that would, and perhaps eloquently, or at least convincingly to many, dispute it, such is the nature of 'spin' and a willingness to dismiss facts in favor of emotion. As for Republicans being racists… I can't stand Barack Obama, I can barely stomach the sound of his voice, his mannerisms, his FACE; I can't stand the guy! Of course this has nothing to do with his political views, polices, or his vision for this Country, I feel this way because of his skin color, I hate him because he's black, because, I'm a racist, **I hate black people**. That is what we Republicans do, we hate anybody who is not white. Now that was a nice quote for someone to use one day to prove how racist Republicans are, and it *would* be used that way, if I was someone influential enough to use and misrepresent to further the liberal agenda. But, the reality is, I don't care, not one bit, about Obama's skin color, or anyone's for that matter. I dislike Obama because he's a Socialist/Globalist out to transform this Country into some other sort of *other* country, and he seeks to dismiss and dismantle our Constitution and the checks and balances of our three-branch system in favor of destructive executive edicts. He lies with careless abandon; his grand ideas are grand failures. He was verbose about Bush's *unpatriotic* 'debt' and its devastating effect on our youth who would be burdened to pay it off, and yet *he* has continued to hit astronomical levels of 'Obama' debt, quite un-patriotically, according to Obama's own standards, and with no concern for the unborn debtors he was borrowing against. Obama railed against "Bush's" wars, and eight years in to the Obama administration, we were still fighting those wars. War is bad when Republicans do it, O.K. when Democrats do it. His belief that we must redistribute wealth from the rich to the poor is a socialist plan that can only reward the *takers* to punish the self-reliant, and ultimately wreak our powerful economic engine. Obama was against gay marriage, until it served him to be for it. The great liberal many decades old 'War on poverty' has failed, with more poor, more dependent on government, more members of a permanent dependent underclass of mostly black and brown Democrats, and more sticking their hand out in favor of improving their lot and making something of themselves. Democrats are in charge of most of America's failing cities, democratic policies continue to fail to bring people out of poverty. Obama sought to increase big government give-a-ways as a method of growing the Democratic voting base. Our founders observed that our Nation could not endure when a majority of our citizens voted for what they could 'get' from government, at the expense of others. We are at that precipice, maybe past it.

So I can't stand Barack Obama, but not because he's black. I, like most Republicans, don't care about a person's color, we measure people based on *character*. One 'proof' if you need it; the most radical and right-wing and **racist** of Republicans, those "Tea Party" supporters, embrace many prominent *black people* into their ranks, and showed much support for Ben Carson, who is even *blacker* than Barack Obama. *Racists*.

The Tea Party: Did you know what their evil 'platform' is? To return to the Constitutional principles of a small unobtrusive and limited Federal Government, to keep taxes low, to allow The States the power to set their own rules as outlined in Article 10, to observe the *limits* The Constitution places on the federal government; to basically "Follow our Constitution." Oh my, The Tea Party is so hateful, and CRAZY.

As *The Tea Party* demonstrates, so much for the myth of *racist Republicans*. Turns out the political party that **obsesses** about skin color, is the *Democratic* party, and liberals in general. Just listen to some liberal media for a few minutes, the *color* of people will be VERY important to them, not so much to Conservatives.

Note: Don't forget, as you doubt this, you're getting this from the source, no spin here, a confessional if you will, from some FOX News listening, Rush Limbaugh liking conservative… but to some, *you can't handle the truth,* it flies in the face of some *narrative* you've been fed, you'd rather dismiss *facts* and cling to *emotion.* These beliefs I'm putting forth here are generally true for conservatives, I've been listening to conservative media for *years* and can tell you this is the same stuff *they* believe. Although liberals will insist that conservatives hate Obama for being black, the *truth* is, conservatives hate Obama for his beliefs, his policies, and his disdain for our Constitution. That is the *truth* about conservatives; I've been watching and listening to them closely, from the *inside* for years, I'm one of THEM, and I know them, and me, no matter what Racheal Maddow says.

Before we leave the 'racist' charge, how about a border wall? Did you know that every major country on earth is pretty picky about letting people into their country? Yes, they are. Did you know that if we just adopted, and enforced, MEXICO'S rules on immigration we'd cure all our illegal immigration problems? We would. Mexico is *tough* on immigration; try showing up in Mexico and see if they give you food stamps, welfare, free school, free healthcare, a place to live, etc., guess what, they'll send you back so quick it'll make your head spin, if they don't lock you up in *prison*. No country can survive by having an open border *and* a generous welfare system, they would go broke, which is what The United States is doing. *(Do you know what our National debt is? We DON'T HAVE ANY MONEY, we **borrow** all the money we give away!)* A border wall, and strict enforcement of our immigration laws, racist? Or *common sense*; like the rest of the world, and MEXICO, we should be very cautious about *who* we let in, and *why*. Barack Obama says **"Build bridges not walls."** He approved building a new, and TALLER, wall around The White House. Hummm.

Republicans hate LGBTQ people. (Lesbian, Gay, Bisexual, Transgender, Queer) That limits the hate quite a bit, liberals would have you believe republicans hate *everybody!* But we'll stick to LGBTQ for now. The Republican party attracts more *religious* people than the Democrats. Biblically, many would point out that sexual deviation from the 'man/woman' model is wrong, in the eyes of God. *I'm* not saying that, but some would. This is one area where 'I' am not the typical Republican. I'm *not* religious. I don't have a dog in *that* fight. This dichotomy between republican and democrat, in *all* areas, but especially when it comes to gender identity, is often set up as one side being caring and compassionate, and one side being hateful, when in fact the *difference* between these political parties *is* really a demonstration of embracing and understanding *diversity*. Diversity is about *differences*. Most of us, especially conservatives, *do* understand and *tolerate* diverse views, or should, for the most part, but we don't have to *champion* some view that is different from ours. We can BE different and believe different things, and be polite about it, and respectful. That is what most of us do, *especially* republicans. Liberals see diversity as a <u>mandate</u> to *embrace* the divergent view, and NOT be different; conservatives understand we will often disagree, we CAN be different, and we can have differing opinions, and that's ok. A republican supporting the 'traditional' view of a man/woman marriage, and believing that allowing marriage outside of this tradition is wrong, is not hateful, it is an example of *diverse* opinions. Liberals are likely to shout down a differing view, have violent demonstrations, try to close down a restaurant whose owner holds such traditional views, rather than accepting our innate human *diversity of opinion*. I don't care who marries who, but I do understand the logic of a government bestowing certain advantages to the long-held and widely accepted traditional view, as a positive advantage to long-term society building. Most of us do realize, even the LGBTQ community, even if they don't like it, that the one-man one-woman model of child-rearing is considered the 'norm' and most of us, conservatives at least, understand it is the *norm* for good reason. It represents the natural scheme of creating a child, and the most stable home environment. Most societies throughout the world have adopted this model since the earliest makings of *modern* society. Courts, therapists, and experts in child-rearing are in general agreement that such a model is preferable. Social experiments that seek to disrupt societal systems that have been in effect for eons is often a dangerous path, especially when the lives of our children WILL suffer the effects of such failed experiments. Compare the out-of-wedlock rates and fatherless homes of blacks and whites, for example, and the difference, and the harm, of not having a father and a mother is obvious.

So we can agree to disagree, especially for those who perceive the *Bible* as the source for such opinions, that some will embrace the LGBTQ lifestyle and some will not. Newsflash, that does not make those who disagree hateful, or bigoted… they have *another view*, one held and accepted by most peoples on Earth, a view that has been the norm for millennia.

Just to diverge a bit, for you "Muslims are just like us" crowd, you know how LGBTQ folks are treated in Muslim countries don't you? Thrown off of buildings, stoned to death, beheaded… etc. So when you LGBTQ supporters also support bringing tons of new Muslims into the country, well, good luck with that. Muslims are NOT like us, in many important respects, especially when it comes to support of LGBTQ issues. Islam is a *different* sort of religion, the only religion on earth that will not tolerate other religions. Move to an Islamic country and try to set up a Christian church. That would have a bad ending. Islam is a religion of forced domination. Just listen to them. Listen to their Holy book.

Back to this marriage thing. I, personally, don't care who marries who, except that I do think the long-held man/woman family structure is best for children and society as a whole. But I'm one who sees the wisdom of the Constitution of *The United States of America*, created by Founders who feared an over-bearing and intrusive Federal monolith, a Constitution whose main goal was to preserve *Individual Freedom* and the rights of individual States, and to rein in and limit in law the powers of the Federal government. As far as issues of marriage, that's probably best left as a *State* issue, the Federal government and the Supreme Court have no jurisdiction here, or shouldn't. Although, it does get legally confusing when states differ in such areas, and people move to some other state, confusing. That divergence from our Constitution, and the Supreme Court acting as the 'Supreme Legislature' has, more than anything else, *created* this turmoil. Bottom line, "marriage" is probably best left out of any *government* hands.

We talked about this, but, like I said, some of this will be repetitive. The issue of transgender people using restrooms becomes a firestorm from time to time. I don't much care about people who are playing the part of a women using the women's restroom, or vice-versa for those women who are acting as men, so what. But there is a safety issue here. Again, this was said earlier, but in case you don't know, there are *creepy* men out there, men who 'get off' on watching women in restrooms, and of course those men who sexually assault women, and, as we blur the lines, or proclaim that anyone who 'feels' like a particular gender can use that gender's restroom when they want to, we've opened that restroom door to all sorts of weirdos. Do you want your young daughters to face some man in the woman's restroom? Those who jump on the transgender restroom issue with both feet need to step off and step back, and stop thinking of everything in terms of their *selfish interests*, and appreciate the danger of letting 'men' into a woman's restroom, locker room, showers, etc. That is a *big* deal, especially when it comes to children and restrooms.

P.S. Just to toss some tinder on your fire. Most phycologists agree that gender confusion is a *psychological problem*, an *illness* if you will, and/or a common, normal, occurrence in young people. Recent studies show that about 90% of boys, and nearly that many girls, will 'grow out' of such gender confusion when they reach puberty. And, that allowing young children to 'decide' which gender to be, especially when the parent allows invasive therapies to alter their natural gender, is child abuse; not me speaking, but experts in the field.

Republicans hate air, and water, and flowers, and puppies. We live in an era where oil is needed to power our economy. We'll advance out of this, technology will advance to the point where some new and clean power source will replace oil, 'fossil fuels' if you will. But we're not there yet. Wind and solar can't do it, yet. And that *new* source, well, we don't have that yet, and so, until we can *actually* replace it, we have a choice. We can be careful and judicious with our use of current sources of energy, and safeguard our environment as we use these sources, or, we can put the *brakes* on our economy. Limiting sources of power from oil and coal will *raise the price of everything*, and will have a massive and negative economic effect on our economy. "Drill baby drill!" is a great strategy right now. That's probably a fair representation of the Republican view on energy. It's a logical view, based on available alternative energy sources and the fact that they cannot 'replace' our reliance on oil, not yet.

Global warming. Did you know that many of the 'scientific facts' in the UN report regarding man-made global warming were falsified? They were. Do you know that more and more highly regarded scientists are distancing themselves from the "man-made global warming" bandwagon? They are.

Think back to high school, remember the "ice age" and the fact that the Earth's 'climate' has *cycles*, that areas covered in ice were once tropical forests, that tropical forests were once covered in ice, that deserts were once seas or forests, etc. You know that right? And yet we now seem to think that the Earth's 'right' temperature and climate is the one we've been used to in our lifetimes? And, you think we can just 'adjust' it by driving a Prius and getting solar panels on your house? You're smarter than that aren't you?

The Democrat view… man-made global warming is the biggest treat there is, I mean we're about to destroy the PLANET as we know it, that's a BIG deal, if it's true. Well, the science *isn't* settled, but even if you believe the most authoritative liberal source, the *United Nations, they say* it would take <u>hundreds of years</u> to see the effect, even if the U.S. were to stop **ALL** its carbon emissions! **ALL** it's carbon emissions. *Hundreds of years to realize any effect.* The more likely reason the liberal federal government is the champion of man-made global warming allies is that the control of C02 emissions would mean the control of EVERYTHING. That's some powerful motivation for big government. Republicans tend to have a pragmatic approach to such global warming hysteria, be cautious and protective of the environment, but within reason continue and expand our use of energy resources to keep our economy growing and keep energy prices low. Seems reasonable.

American is great!
Vs. *We need to be knocked down a few pegs.*

For too many of us we vote for the candidate that rings our Pavlovian bell, the one who identifies with 'our' *issues*; gay rights, abortion, minimum wage, free college, free healthcare, stick it to the rich, whatever. We have no sense of Nationalism, no ultimate concern about how our vote will affect our *Nation*; no *pride* in America. Too many vote primarily in their self-interest, so that they can 'get theirs.' Our Founders knew that when the majority simply voted for who 'gave them the most stuff' we were done as a Country. Most of us who think little about the ultimate fate of our Country, and who focus on our *personal* issues, may one day be surprised that we have truly 'transformed' this Nation into something quite different, with far-reaching and negative implications upon our *freedom*. Too many consider themselves critical thinkers, and yet vote for an Obama, support a Hillary or a Bernie, who are all bent on making this Nation into some *other*, something quite foreign to the vision of our Founders, and quite alien to the percepts of our Constitution. So much for critical thinking. If you voted for Obama once, perhaps out of *white guilt*, you were a fool. If you voted for him again, after what he'd *done*, a *traitor*. We are a Nation founded on personal freedom. *We The People* means something profound. *We* control our government, it does not control us, at least that is what our Constitution intended.

As we concede our personal freedoms to a Federal leviathan, and allow the continued erosion of our Constitution to be the target of an activist liberal Supreme Court, we watch freedom disappear. Some see a particular candidate and say they could never vote for them, they did something or said something that was too much, too off the rails, too contrary to their personal beliefs. This was occurring as of the writing of this book with Donald Trump. Conservatives are the *majority* in this country, you wouldn't know that from the liberal media, but they are. Obama was elected because Republicans couldn't get themselves to vote for Romney, millions of Republicans stayed home, and, we got Obama. Millions of Republicans in the "Never Trump" movement were prepared to repeat that mistake in 2016, getting Hillary in exchange for their supposed moral high-ground. I won't go into all the positions of Donald Trump, but virtually every one makes *factual* sense, and virtually every one of those positions is deemed hateful, racist, homophobic, Islamophobic, and requiring of violent emotional protests by liberals. *Fact vs. Emotion.*

P.S. Above when I called some of you fools for voting for Obama, and then traitors; I'll bet you have no idea what I'm talking about. I'll bet in your world Obama has been WONDERFUL, and has, like some messiah, saved The United States from ruin. This is the problem with listening to too much of any one media, there is much news they won't report. The liberal media is an arm of the Democratic party, or vice/versa, we do NOT have an independent mainstream media to tell us the truth, they WILL slant the news and fail to report the stories that don't follow their narrative. If you do a 'little' research about Obama's failures, you'll find a rabbit hole that your liberal media never let you go down. The Iran deal (insuring Iran WILL get a nuclear weapon soon.) Eric Holder's gun-running into Mexico (Fast and Furious), Russian Uranium… and the list of Obama scandals goes on and on, and, most liberals have NO idea.

*P.S. #2 Well, updating this book a bit, half the country got it right, and our new President has begun acting upon his campaign promises. If liberals can just relax (don't count on it) they'll see a real President lead. The idea of a non-politician just getting stuff done, should be quite refreshing. I for one am SICK of Democrats, **and** Republicans. Donald Trump will most likely think like a businessman, getting things done, not* *as a typical politician who generally supports some status quo. But, the democrats will not go easily, and are proving that they will fight The President every day, at every turn, on everything he attempts to do. So much for accepting the results of a Presidential election. Another problem, the republicans. President Trump is a non-politician, and that doesn't sit well with politicians, of either party, even his own party is obstructing the new President; isn't politics wonderful! No, it isn't, it's a dirty business, and life-time politicians is NOT the model this country was founded on. Term limits, good luck getting the politicians to limit themselves.*

Abortion.

This is another hot button issue where liberals tend to repeat some *"Republicans hate women"* mantra, while often not even understanding the basics of abortion. In the first trimester, the baby doesn't look like much, it has a beating heart, but it's not very impressive, not very *human* looking on an ultrasound. In the first trimester the baby can simply be *suctioned out*, or the woman can be chemically induced to hemorrhage and the baby dies and comes out that way, by bleeding out clots of blood and 'tissue.' But, in the second trimester, well, that's a 'real' baby, it has all its parts, it *looks* like a baby on an ultrasound, and an abortion at this stage means reaching in with forceps, grabbing arms and legs, ripping them off, then crushing the little skull and pulling out all the little pieces. Liberals tend to say "It's a woman's body, she should be able to do what she wants with it." That *sounds* good, but is there a *limit*. There currently IS a limit, women aren't allowed to kill their baby *after* it is born, simply because it's *part of their body*, and they aren't allowed to kill their baby the *day before* it's born, again, murder. And we can count backwards… until we reach some age where it IS OK to kill their baby, currently that's up to the second trimester, when they can have the fully formed living baby ripped apart piece by piece. Abortion is one area where there probably can be no universally acceptable 'middle ground.' To some, a woman should be able to kill her baby whenever she wants to, and perhaps, however she wants to. To others, killing a baby is murder. Exactly 'when' the forming baby is worthy of the status of 'baby' or 'human' is not something that will be settled any time soon. And so, those who seek to place *some restrictions* on abortion, will be *haters* of women. Those who want to leave the killing of babies largely unrestricted, will be *champions,* who won't let some man tell them what they can or can't do with their bodies. Who's right? Again, we can't always comprise, we can't always reach some middle ground that makes both sides happy, such is the nature of diverse opinions. Oh, and for most of you, the uninformed, did you know that *Margaret Sanger* founded *Planned Parenthood* in order to kill **black** babies? Of course that's BS, of course it's some conservative *lie…* or, maybe you should look that one up. Abortion kills *mostly* black babies, by a HUGE margin, so for all you "Black lives matter" ~~morons~~ people, I guess you don't *really* believe that either. There I go, calling you names, well…

White privilege.

Please. If you're white, did you grow up with black children in your class at school? Probably. Through all our school years we share the classroom with all sorts of other kids, of different religions, with different socio and economic backgrounds, and of different colors. Did all the kids in your classrooms get the same books? Did they take the same tests? Did we all have the same standards for receiving grades in those classes? Did all our parents have the same opportunity to make sure we did our homework and study? Yes, yes, yes, and yes. And yet we're told that just being *white* is something you should apologize for, that you should be punished for, you should be reprimanded for, and, in the end, whatever you do, you're *still* a racist, *because you're white.* Shame on you! And the black kids who did poorly in school, that wasn't *their* fault, it was some white person's fault. This is an example of the liberal OBSESSION with color. Where a conservative tends to measure people on their *character* and accomplishments, liberals tend to excuse poor performance and blame skin color, excuse criminal behavior and blame skin color, and liberals tend to increase dependence on government give-a-ways because having dark skin means you can't help it, you can't make it, whitey is keeping you down, you deserve some Robin Hood "Take from the rich and give to the poor" because, you have dark skin. And of course that's why black and brown people make up most of our prison population, because of white racism. Please.

The United States of America. Picture a world where people are judged on their *actions* not their skin color. A world where people of *every* race, creed, and color live together, work together, play together, happily; this world where *all* can work if they choose to, where *opportunity* is shared, where everyone can climb the ladder as high as they *choose* to according to their ability and their drive. Open your eyes; it's the world we live in.

Is it your *skin color* or your *actions* when you are viewed negatively for rioting and looting, when your *cause* is based on *race* not reason, *color* and not common sense, when your 'community' embraces "Hands up don't shoot" and "Black lives matter" when black lives *always* mattered, and when his hands *weren't* up. Is it your *color* or your *actions* that make white people shake their heads?

Are they 'haters' for believing in their God, for seeing a sin and yet loving the lesbian, gay, bisexual, and transgender. Should those whose beliefs are *different* than you be driven out of business, become the brunt of protests, become demonized because they *dare to believe* the words of their God? The hearts of those who see the sin are most often *open hearts* full of love, whose crime is that they *disagree*. What is *tolerance*, what is *diversity*, what is *compassion*, if not to *embrace* those who disagree? When we **insist** on *conversion* to our ideas, when we **force** one group to abandon *their beliefs* and accept *ours*, we become the *terrorist* not the *tolerant*. My goal here has been to place our emphasis on facts, not emotion, as we form our views.

THE LIBERAL BRAIN:

It's clear to conservatives that liberals must be crazy. Turns out that isn't far from the truth, there does seem to be a defect in the liberal brain involving the prefrontal cortex.

This information from *Wikipedia* on the following pages discusses the **results of adult damage to various parts of the brain and frontal cortex**, and *the decision-making results of such brain damage.*

It is logical to see these specific examples as a window into understanding such brain *defects* in a more general sense. Our brains are not mature until we are about **25 years old**, it is during these formative years that a failure to 'use' critical thinking may doom us to live with a miswired brain, a brain incapable of proper logical and fact-based analysis, which may last a lifetime. Science seems to believe that this defect may explain the twisted and illogical nature of *liberal thinking*.

We don't necessarily have to undergo *physical* trauma to the brain to *damage* it. The early development of our brain, and the later adolescent and young adult maturing process of the prefrontal cortex, can result in similar *damage*. As we mature, the brain naturally **prunes away** little-used connections. If we are not raised as *critical thinkers*, and <u>practice</u> *informed reasoning* while we are young, we may lose those abilities in some areas, permanently. If neuro connections are missing, or miswired during this maturation period, the result is a less than optimal functioning portion of the brain, ***with similar defects in logic, emotion, and decision-making as might be experienced with physical trauma to the brain.***

This revelation may provide the missing link to understanding the strange and contradictory behaviors of the liberal mind in some areas, and specifically in some *subjects*, in the presence of an otherwise functional and even otherwise highly intelligent and logical individuals. Remember, if you spend your formative years in an environment where both sides of issues are *not* examined, where some liberal professor 'tells you what to think' and you simply adopt that view, well, you haven't thought it out, you haven't used all those neuropathways that let you *reason*, to think *critically*, and ultimately those little used pathways are pruned away, and you are left with a brain *incapable* of such reasoned evaluation of differing views in certain areas, *a defective prefrontal cortex.*

This list details some specific areas of thinking and reasoning defects when *damage to the prefrontal cortex has occurred.* Some bells should ring here, look in the mirror, or at the reflection of someone close to you…

Do these signs of a malfunctioning prefrontal cortex seem familiar to you? **Do they mirror the behavior of the liberal mind?**

*Impaired **moral judgment***

*Severe impairments in personal and social **decision-making***

***Impaired capacity to learn from their mistakes**, making the same decisions again and again even though they lead to negative consequences*

*Seem to be **blind to the future consequences of their actions***

*More **easily influenced** by misleading advertising*

*There is a gap in reasoning when applying the same moral principles to similar situations in their own lives. The result is that people make **decisions that are inconsistent with their self-professed moral values***

*More likely to endorse **self-serving actions that break moral rules or cause harm to others***

*Causes **failure in using correct moral emotion***

*Causes impairments of **behavioral control and decision making***

***Impulsive** murderers have decreased activity in the prefrontal cortex*

*Lower activation in the prefrontal cortex is also correlated with **antisocial behavior***

*Show defects both in **emotional response and emotion regulation***

*They show markedly **reduced social emotions such as compassion, shame and guilt**. These are emotions that are closely associated with moral values. Patients also exhibit **poorly regulated anger and frustration tolerance** in certain circumstances*

*Changes such as **lack of empathy, irresponsibility, and poor decision making**. These traits are similar to psychopathic personality traits*

That's something to think about...

If we look at a political demonstration by liberals, we often see extreme anger issues on display, lack of tolerance, lack of control, lack of empathy as they burn and destroy the property of others, poor decision making, irresponsible and illegal behavior, even physical assaults on those they disagree with, and a seeming disregard for the consequences of their actions. Those protestors often wear masks, looking much like the terrorists who practice similar tactics. We see many of those signs we just discussed, that indicate pre-frontal cortex brain issues. And, interestingly, at a political demonstration put on by conservatives, we see little or none of that. It is the interaction with liberal protestors where these issues arise. Interesting.

Critical thinking homework for liberals:

List some specific conservative view in this book, and write a brief rebuttal on this page and the next, proving how wrong that view was, using facts if possible. That should be a challenge. ↓

Chapter Three

"The Tea Party":
A Liberal Rorschach test

"The Rorschach test, also known as the Rorschach inkblot test, the Rorschach technique, or simply the inkblot test, is a psychological test in which subjects' perceptions of inkblots are recorded and then analyzed using psychological interpretation, complex algorithms, or both. Some psychologists use this test to examine a person's personality characteristics and emotional functioning. It has been employed to detect underlying thought disorder, especially in cases where patients are reluctant to describe their thinking processes openly. The test is named after its creator, Swiss psychologist Hermann Rorschach." **Wikipedia**

The *Rorschach* analogy is used here in respect to liberals and their perceptions of *The Tea Party*. It's quite interesting really to use "The Tea Party" like a Rorschach test, to examine the personality characteristics and emotional functioning of a liberal. Although there is some risk here, I'd advise that you *do* try this at home. Other books have delved into liberalism as a thought disorder or disease, and when you look at liberalism in that way it does become easier to understand it. Liberalism at its core *is* a sickness, with its pathology spread through *generalization, group-think, pie-in-the-sky paradigms, naivety, anti-American teachings, and guilt.* For you liberals reading this, if you keep reading, you may discover something about yourself, and, maybe you aren't too far gone, *maybe* you can recover.

The term *Lemming* to describe a liberal is apt; they quickly follow in line eager to spread their flimsy diatribe to others willing to abandon common sense, statistics, or historical fact.

And so, we'll discuss *The Tea Party* in terms of its perception by liberals, and we'll discover something profound, the fact that liberals do indeed share an *"underlying thought disorder"* pathology that is quickly revealed by asking one of them this simple question, ***"What do you think of The Tea Party?"***

Asking your liberal friend or family member this question will quickly expose something quite fascinating, you will hear high *emotion* coupled with flimsy, distorted, or non-existent facts. When pushed to supply *factual* evidence of this Tea Party hatred, you will ultimately encounter an escalation in *emotion*, and ultimately a *disengagement*. The liberal will not be able to support their negative view of The Tea Party, the sound bites they parrot from their media quickly expose themselves to be just that, *emotional* statements devoid of facts. This negative view of liberal thought isn't new, here's a bit of history:

"If there is ever a fascist takeover in America, it will come not in the form of storm troopers kicking down doors but with lawyers and social workers saying. I'm from the government and I'm here to help."
— Jonah Goldberg

I have to tell you, you know, it's part of reporting this case, this election, the feeling most people get when they hear Barack Obama's speech. My, I felt this thrill going up my leg.
— "Journalist" Chris Matthews

The trouble with our Liberal friends is not that they're ignorant; it's just that they know so much that isn't so.
Ronald Reagan

If you have always believed that everyone should play by the same rules and be judged by the same standards, that would have gotten you labeled a radical 60 years ago, a liberal 30 years ago and a racist today.
Thomas Sowell

'Be faithful to your roots' is the liberal version of 'Stay in your ghetto.'
Mason Cooley

Swing voters are more appropriately known as the 'idiot voters' because they have no set of philosophical principles. By the age of fourteen, you're either a Conservative or a Liberal if you have an IQ above a toaster.
Ann Coulter

A liberal is a man who will give away everything he doesn't own.
Frank Dane

If you're a liberal, anything you say is protected. If you're a conservative, anything you say is hateful.
Laura Schlessinger

A conservative is a liberal who got mugged the night before.
Frank Rizzo

Let's be honest about this; the liberal agenda with failed stimulus plans and government entitlement programs is crippling our economy and our quality of life.
Alveda King

It is the liberal philosophy, not the conservative one, that views humans as selfish automatons.
Allen West

The difference between a contemporary liberal and a socialist is that to a liberal the most beautiful word in the English language is 'forbidden', whereas to a socialist the most beautiful word is 'compulsory'.
John McCarthy

A liberal will cut off your leg so he can hand you a crutch.
Jim Brown

In the liberal remake of 'Casablanca,' the police captain comes upon the scene of the shooting and orders his men to 'round up the usual weapons.' It's always the weapon and never the shooter.
Charles Krauthammer

A liberal mind is a mind that is able to imagine itself believing anything.
Max Eastman

Well, I'm a libertarian conservative, so I believe in limited government/maximum individual freedom.
John Bolton

There is something that underlies some of these liberal opinions that is vitally important when trying to understand the disconnect between liberal and conservative thought, *The Constitution of The United States of America.* For the most part liberals will wax eloquent on their devotion to it, love for our Country, and their patriotism, all while applauding each new erosion of State's rights, each new federal tentacle that strangles personal freedom, and each new dictum from on high that makes new law with the wave of an Executive pen, all in clear violation of that 'sacred' Constitution they often claim to support. If you strip away the veneer built on lies and misdirection, you find the heart of a liberal overflowing with *contempt* for that Constitution. Actions speak louder than words, and the actions of the last liberal administration was one intent on usurping our Constitution.

The fact that liberals glom onto whatever media direction they are given is embarrassing to watch. The confederate flag issue is a perfect example of the *Rahm Emanuel/Obama* strategy to capitalize on tragedy to advance their agenda.

Rahm Emanuel: *"You never want a serious crisis to go to waste. And what I mean by that is an opportunity to do things you think you could not do before."*

A racist maniac kills people in a church, and because a photo found in his belongings shows him holding a confederate flag, that flag must be *banished* from society. And the liberal lemmings follow right in line. They only need enough time to put down their rainbow flag to follow the next media/political *cause of the day*. Let's remove all Confederate statues, etc., let's erase whatever history doesn't suit our current cause. Let's re-write the history of the Civil War. Let's make that Confederate flag the symbol of overt racism and hate, and then banish it from society.

This Politically Correct bandwagon becomes too noisy for most 'typical' conservatives, who then seek to add *their* voice to the deafening din, in order to gain some imaginary favor with the media or some supposed future *swing voter*. The few who remain strong, determined, and steadfast in their convictions then become the new radicals, out of step with this sudden societal evolution. The lemming line grows, and at the end of the line we see those weak conservatives trying to keep in step, and only this new 'Tea Party' standing on the sidelines watching the democrats *and* republicans marching by.

Give the liberal machine a slogan and they will run with it.

"I can't breathe"   *"Hands up don't shoot"*   *"The gentle giant"*

Our social media environment is the perfect vehicle to spread lies and manipulate vapid youth. *Facebook, Twitter,* and *Instagram*, are the new *Pravda*. Our young people smile dimwittedly while 'liking' the latest propaganda, and feeling like they are part of a generation evolving quickly into this newly 'transformed' and *improved* nation. Our founders worried that ignorant masses and those whose motivations for political change depend on who will *give them* the most stuff, would doom our Republic. We seem to be living in the throes of this predicted decline.

Chapter Four

"We The People"
United

It took decades. *It* came in bits here and there, the constant political banter, TV shows and commercials trying to *normalize* what was not normal, the comments on radio and television programs, the ads, all intent on changing long-held thoughts and beliefs. The barrage came on sitcoms, documentaries, reality shows, social media, and the *news*, some we recognized as *out of the mainstream* and some were well disguised, more insidious, the messages that came to us almost subliminally. It also came in our school books, our lesson plans, the liberal network of Professors and other teachers marching with the new agenda to alter history, to create young people eager to toss out the old and bring in the new. Our youth were given limited and skewed information on our founding, on our Nation, on our culture. And in the end we, millions and millions of us, were changed, our *values* were changed, and the essence of our *Founding* has been lost. We allowed our schools to delete history or revise it. *We The People* are becoming a *different people,* and we may not like the *transformation* when it is complete.

"We The People" is an important concept. That little phrase is the heart of what we are and how we became a Nation, United. But, we have lost sight of our founding. Our children have a minimal and warped knowledge of our Founders, and of our Constitution, and of what it means to be an *American*. The 'Global Neighborhood' *sounds* good, but so much of the rest of the world is NOT like us, they do not share our founding on principles of individual *freedom*, we are rightfully and significantly *different*, and *exceptional*, in a good way.

The thing that has been transforming us is an *agenda*. Just what this agenda includes and who is at the heart of it is a tangled web, and beyond the scope of this little book. But this new vision of America *is* being formalized, we are perhaps at the epicenter in this moment in time of this transformation, a vital turning point. This new vision is a vision of a *different* America, it is based on a warped understanding of our founders and our founding. This *new* America is one built on the false premise of a twisted world view. A view that sees something better out there, some *other* form of government, some *other* values, some *other* economic system, some possible new world more like… well, that's the problem, if you were to ask these world revisionists what model they prefer you would begin to see a crack in a very delicate veneer, you would begin to understand that they seek some *other* system yet to be disclosed, they are ready to bulldoze *this* down, and see what happens.

Note: I should stop here for a moment. Since this book was first written, things have changed. I've updated some of this, some not. Although we are in the very beginning of a new era, we are beginning it. Obama is gone, and we have a new President. Now where were we?

Most of those who want to *change* America don't know what they want it to become, they only believe that what we *are* is flawed. These decades of indoctrination have left them believing that Capitalism is bad, profit is bad, corporations are bad, Wall Street is bad, rich people are bad, the owners of companies are bad, oil is bad, Republicans are bad, The Tea Party is bad, George Bush (of course) is bad, the 1% is bad, wanting to have rules about abortion is bad, Donald Trump is bad. Religion is mostly bad, having borders is bad, the police are bad, prisons are bad, but Cuba is good, Che Guevara is cool, drugs are good, Democrats are good, Obama is good, Occupy Wall Street (whoever they are) is good, abortion is good, raising the minimum wage is ALWAYS good, allowing EVERYBODY into this Country is good (Build bridges not walls), Muslims are good, big government is good (especially when they promise to take more money from those who have and

46

give it to those who have less), and of course the rich 1% that *they like* are good (movie stars, singers, Kardashians, etc.) They are not only looking through rose-colored glasses but they have the wrong prescription, their world view is *fuzzy*, to say the least.

We'll look at some of those blurred visions and try to bring them into focus. In the end it is my hope that this little book can do something that Thomas Paine's *Common Sense* did, to a few at least, to make us see things through the lens of common sense, to allow us to put aside those decades of manipulation and to see what is, not what we are told we see.

In 1776 Thomas Paine wrote a little pamphlet, it was called "Common Sense."

That little pamphlet was perhaps *the* turning point in our American Revolution, in it Thomas Paine simplified the concerns of the time and brought a summary of political matters to the common man.

Words matter, they are the stuff of thoughts, and thoughts the stuff of action. Lies have great power to influence those who take to lies to easily, but when the truth is exposed, we most often find at its heart, *common sense.*

Note, it's not *all* your fault if you've been wearing those rose-colored glasses, or if you've fallen victim to political and media manipulation, they've been good at it, it's infected many of us, nearly half of us it seems. So take a moment to remove those glasses, to see with *your* eyes, to hear with *your* ears, and push aside, if just for a few dozen pages, what you've been *told* to see and hear. We all have common sense but sometimes it can be clouded, sometimes those who would use us for their nefarious plans can do so without us realizing it, more often they realize exactly what they're doing. But we can cut the strings of the puppeteer and walk free, and in the end we can see those who seek to *control* us and to transform America for what they are, *evil.*

The message for many black people should be clear by now, the liberals want your support, they *count* on it, they *buy it* with welfare and food stamps and promises, they demonize conservatives who talk about pulling you up and out of poverty.

The Democrats like you where you are, beholding to them, *their* permanent underclass who will be permanently held down by whitey. Newsflash, most of our failed cities with high black unemployment, crime, poor schools, etc., are, and have for decades, *been run by Democrats*. But they *expect* your vote, they count on it, *they like you where you are*. If you climbed that ladder and made a better life for yourself, well, you wouldn't need them now would you.

What happened to us?

The truth can be hard to come by. Too many of us have become accustomed to lies, they have come loose and easy from the lips of those we should be able to trust. Our media, whose grand and noble purpose is to uncover and expose the *truth*, has failed us with their overt participation in the manufacture and dissemination of *lies*. They are an arm of their liberal political party, or perhaps the puppeteer, moving and manipulating that political party, and either way, willing to distort the truth to serve their liberal ends.

In my book *"The Poison of POLITICAL CORRECTNESS"* I discussed *Critical Thinking* and outlined some lies that dominated our headlines using the false assumptions of Political Correctness and the tool of *race* to influence the thinking of many…

Critical thinking is directly tied to *Political Correctness*. Those who use Political Correctness as a means to manipulate people are quickly exposed when Critical Thinking is employed. Critical Thinking is the light to the cockroach that is Political Correctness.

Trayvon Martin, you know, if Barack Obama had a son he would have looked like Trayvon. Humm, really? I guess Barack Obama thinks all black people look alike. Do you remember this case? Trayvon Martin was coming home from the store, he had *Skittles* and an "Iced Tea."

Fast forward... George Zimmerman thinks Trayvon is acting suspicious, he calls the police, but before the police arrive Trayvon ends up on top of Zimmerman beating him and Zimmerman pulls out his gun and shoots Trayvon. Trayvon dies. Witnesses testify that Trayvon was on top of Zimmerman, beating him, and the jury decides Zimmerman was justified in shooting him.

Trayvon, was just a *kid* who went to the store to buy some candy and some iced tea. For TV the media chose a picture of Trayvon several years younger, smiling, not the more *gangsta* looking current photo of Trayvon. Why'd they pick *that* picture? Well, it wasn't iced tea, it was *Arizona Watermelon Fruit Juice Cocktail.* Did you know that Arizona Watermelon Fruit Juice Cocktail, a bag of Skittles, and simple cough syrup make a codeine-based drink called "lean?" Did you hear that on the news? There's an entire online subculture devoted to the use of "lean," which Trayvon was familiar with. There are online posts from Trayvon where he says he could make some "fire-ass lean" using cough syrup, skittles, and Arizona Watermelon Fruit Juice Cocktail. Humm, those were the two items he was heading home with, two-thirds of the ingredients needed to make "lean." Just an innocent smiling kid heading home with Skittles and Iced Tea? He didn't do ANYTHING, the racist Zimmerman just shot him, for no reason. I hate racists.

Trayvon's autopsy showed liver damage in this otherwise healthy young 18-year-old that are consistent with the kind of damage that excessive "lean" usage causes to the liver. Humm. And the psychological symptoms associated with the use of "lean," extreme physical aggression and paranoia. Humm. You heard all that on the news right?

Another case... *Michael Brown* in Ferguson, Missouri, you know, the guy who just stole a few cigars and was 'gunned down' by a racist cop even though he had his hands up and said "Don't shoot", remember? Well, except that after stealing those cigars and pushing around the store owner he refused to listen to the police officer who told him to get out of the street, and then Michael Brown got into a fight with the officer while the officer sat in his car, trying to take the officer's gun, and then Brown ran away but then turned and charged at the officer, and the officer shot him, and he died. Did you know that the evidence showed he never had his hands up, he *did* try to take the officer's gun, and he *did* rush at the officer, "head down like a football player." I hate racist witnesses, and racist people doing autopsy reports, and... oh, those witnesses were black, and the Obama administration and the black Attorney General did their own autopsy and did their own investigation of all the facts, and THEY also agreed that the police officer was justified in shooting Brown, oh.

Eric Garner on Staten Island, he was just selling illegal cigarettes on the sidewalk when racist cops jumped on him, and he said he couldn't breathe, but they handcuffed him, and he died. They didn't have to do that, he was just selling illegal cigarettes, they didn't need to jump on him and restrain him just because he wouldn't listen to the police and he resisted getting arrested. Racists. They could have just let him sell his cigarettes, why would the police have to arrest someone committing a crime and then handcuff somebody resisting arrest, why? Racists, yup, that's why.

Racist cops. Cops hate black people. Black lives don't matter. Cops get up in the morning and go out looking for black people to harass or kill. Fucking cops. Racist country. The jails are *full* of black and brown people. Black and brown people are arrested a LOT more than white people. White people get off; black people go to jail. Have you ever watched an episode of COPS? The racists who make that show fill it up with cops arresting black people, why don't they show more white people getting arrested? Because the cops only go after black people, *racists*. Or, do more black people get arrested because more black people are committing more crime than white people? NO, I'm sure that's just some racist who wants you to believe that!

Does any of that make you think? Maybe it makes you think *differently*? Maybe you begin to see a pattern, a pattern of media and government manipulation? A manipulation of your culture or your race? Humm. Critical Thinking is about relying on *facts* not *emotion*. Get a T-Shirt, it says "Hands up don't shoot" or "I can't breathe" or "Black lives matter" because you're making a statement, you're standing up for... uh, you're making a statement about racism? Or you're making another statement, something like "I'm easily manipulated, I'm *not* a Critical Thinker."

It's Politically Correct right now to forget about facts, "Hands up don't shoot."

It's Politically Correct to believe that *racism* is what fills up our prisons with black and brown people.

It's Politically Correct to blame the *police* for crime, and for arrests of innocent black people. Innocent? You think? Really? The police just make stuff up, the people they arrest aren't *really* drug dealers, or thieves, or guilty of some crime? The prisons are full of innocent people? You believe that?

We don't need to ascribe to some wild conspiracy theory, the essence of what's happening is clear. Someone *is* pitting us against each other. For political reasons? To gain power? To control us? Something is going on behind the scenes. We are being manipulated for a *purpose*, someone, some organization, some political party, some agenda is benefiting from growing tension between the races and growing animosity toward our local police. I like chess, but not when I'm one of the pieces.

All those cases listed, and the truth about them; Trayvon Martin, Michael Brown, Eric Gardner; I'll bet you liberals don't believe it. You most likely think that George Zimmerman is a racist and he simply murdered Trayvon, you most likely think that Michael Brown was murdered by the cop, and that the cops who choked Eric Gardner were racists that wanted to kill him… the facts and the results of jury trials usually don't matter to liberals; they'll stick with their *feelings* about such cases. Facts are so, *racist*.

When we stop to think for ourselves, we often come to a frightening realization that what is *real* is quite different than the narrative coming from our most influential media sources. They, much of the "mainstream" media, has allowed itself to abandon "journalism" and the pursuit of truth, in favor of serving a political cause. Journalists choose to write stories that reflect *their* views instead of exposing truth and reporting facts. "Journalists" are caught using misleading editing to influence *news* stories. We are left with a world where images and sound bites are used to support a particular political agenda, a media that is more like those state sponsored news outlets of the Soviet Union than the unbiased source of fact that most Americans expect.

Chapter Five:

Facts have a curious way of being true

First, I don't like Republicans. And, I don't like Democrats. I don't even like "Independents" since it seems to me that says you don't really have any *core* principles, you could sway from supporting Republicans or Democrats from moment to moment, election to election, based on… hum, personality, on who has the best smile? These parties *do* stand for something, they have core principles, and have differing views on various social and political topics. I'm all for voting for the *person* but these *people* have some core beliefs, and I'd like them to match up with mine, as much as possible, especially those views that support America, and our Constitution.

So, what do you think of this?

• Republicans support rich corporations and greed, and that's bad.

• A vibrant economy depends on rich corporations and greed, and we like a vibrant economy, so Republicans are good.

• Greed is never good, what's wrong with you?

• Greed is really a desire for profit, that's the whole basis of a company, to make money, to succeed, to expand, to make more money, etc., Capitalism is what has made the American economy great, what's wrong with you?

• Democrats are for the *people*. Corporations are out for *themselves*. Republicans support corporations, Democrats don't?

• Successful corporations only exist because of the *people* that make them work, that company "didn't build that."

• Did you ever get a job from a poor person?

These sorts of arguments, with someone on each side of the issue, can be made with topics such as religion, race, abortion, oil, illegal immigration, student loans, healthcare, you name it. And in the end people take sides, and someone comes out as the villain, and we decide which political party best stands with *us* and shares our point of view.

But there's a problem, just like those bullet points on the preceding page, these issues, such as greed, corporations, and Capitalism are NOT Republican or Democratic issues. We've been manipulated to think of such disagreements in those political terms. *Both* of the political parties thrive in this Capitalistic society, they *both* support big corporations, and they *both* realize our economic system exists *because of* corporate profit motive (greed if you like) and they both continue policies that encourage Capitalism.

Note: Capitalism is WHY The United States is the envy of much of the world, duh.

But, if the Republicans had their way there'd be *less* government intrusion into business, and there would probably be more small businesses created, more ability for existing small businesses to remain profitable and to grow, and even more *profit* being made. Profit equals more taxes to the federal government, and profit and expansion means *more* jobs for more people. Democrats seem to like *more restrictions* on businesses and *more government intrusion*, more regulation, hence less small business creation, less profit and expansion, and fewer jobs created. In the end they support Capitalism, *profit*, but they want more *control* of it. So, both parties are FOR big business, despite the image portrayed by Democrats; but, the Democratic party has a different *approach* to business, they want to assert control over it by imposing rules and regulations from *Big Brother* who *must* <u>know</u>

better than the business owner. The political parties are different, but not in the way they paint themselves. The age of Trump should demonstrate that a pro-business, less regulation, less intrusive government policy is a boost to our economic engine, and that job growth and prosperity does follow such policies. We'll see.

There was a time when the Industrial Age was running rampant and out of control, and the government played a useful role in reining in the *profit at any price* mentality of some. But we have gone past the growing pains of the industrial age, and worker's rights and safe working conditions have become the norm. The Federal government stepped into the role that should have been filled by the State, in the name of *the worker*, and there was a time for that, but now the Federal government should step back, into its proper place and leave that role to the States, or, be *forced* to step back. Free up the market place, and Capitalism thrives.

A proper look at big business, corporations, Capitalism, profit, should allow one to see what makes America different, and why America is the global powerhouse it is. Some massive left turn toward Socialism isn't the answer, just ask those who have come to the United States from a Socialist country. But our young people swoon at the rhetoric of a Bernie Sanders; *free* this, *free* that, *equal* everything. Those young people who "Feel the Bern" do prove one thing, that our education system has FAILED. History, especially the evils of history, such as Socialism, only need repeat itself if we don't learn its lessons, and our youth have NOT.

If we just tax the rich more, and more, and more… we can pay for all the FREE stuff, just ask Bernie. The rich shouldn't be so rich, their wealth should be limited. Just how much money should anyone be able to make, or keep in the bank? Or, is our country a great economic engine BECAUSE of the rich? And, in the end, with this "Rich Vs. Poor" argument, when the rich have made too much, when they're *too* rich, they should GIVE THEIR MONEY TO **YOU**. Humm. You, who just *exists*, you didn't earn anything, but **YOU** should have the money earned by those who worked for it? Humm. Interesting *logic*. Take from the rich and give to the poor only works for a while, and then you run out of the rich, you kill the incentive to *become* rich, to succeed, when success means you become the cash cow for those who choose to 'take yours' over 'make something of themselves.' Socialism doesn't bring everyone UP, it ends up bringing those who have, DOWN. "Level the playing field" means make everyone equally miserable. The big winners in Socialism, are the elite Socialists in charge.

And so, all this HATEFUL speech, a whole little book full of it, terrible. *The border, guns, war, the criminal justice system, racism, sexism, LGBTQ issues, capitalism, socialism, race, abortion, oil, global warming, healthcare, welfare, "free" school, the minimum wage,* and the list goes on. Conservatives and Liberals, Republicans and Democrats; they see the world *quite* differently. Yes, we do.

HOLD EVERYTHING!

Muslims. Islam.

We almost forgot THIS! "The religion of peace." Muslims aren't dangerous, they just want a better life. They're just like us. Islam is a peaceful religion. ISIS, and the Islamic State, isn't *Islamic*. Muslim terrorists are NOT Muslims. No religion allows the killing of innocents. Blah, blah, blah, blah, blah. There's something wrong here, somebody isn't paying attention.

"Radical Islam." President Obama banned that phrase for nearly eight years, the terrorists weren't attacking us in the *name of Islam*. Shouting "Allahu Akbar" (God is great) and **telling us** they were doing this in the name of their religion, what do *they* know. And Muslim refugees, millions of them, and ISIS **telling us** they would use this influx of refugees to get ISIS members into the west, ha, what do *they* know. Mostly young men, young Muslims, from radical America-hating countries, of course they'll be "just like us" and peaceful, and they'll respect other religions and other beliefs, and they'll get a job, and they'll want to become Germans or French or Italians, or Americans, sure, of course they will. And Donald Trump, agreeing with the CIA and Homeland Security and the FBI that these people pose a real risk, what a bunch of Islamophobic racist haters. A half-million crimes and counting committed by these Muslim *refugees*; rape, murder, beheadings, killing children while they sleep, and all the rest. They're just like us. There's something interesting about "*Radical* Islam" it looks a LOT like "Islam."

Should we stop pouring these questionable Muslims into Europe and the U.S., at least until we can figure out how to properly screen them and figure out just how many we should allow in? Of course not, that would make us *haters*.

Note: The previous paragraph, about slowing down immigration from terrorist countries; as of the writing of this book, that has happened. A campaign promise fulfilled, sort of, as the liberal activist courts stand in the way, or try to. We'll see how this all works out, but trying to make sure we don't bring people into America that *hate* America, seems like a good idea to about half of us Americans.

I could list a LONG list here… of all the attacks of the last few years by Muslims on the west, and that list is *long*, and lots of people died, but *Islam is the religion of peace*, so I guess that list is wrong, it was probably put together by some Muslim hater.

America's struggle against Islam is historic, our country *began* its early history with an epic battle against Muslim pirates in Tripoli. *Churchill* famously pointed out the dangers of Islam; this isn't new.

If you don't 'get' that we have a Muslim problem in the *world*, and a BIG one, and that bringing this Muslim problem INTO our country is a BIG mistake, well, you are trying *really* hard to be a good liberal, you must have *two* pair of rose-colored glasses on.

There's much evidence to support the fact that somebody (liberals) have some 'brain issues.' (We talked about that earlier) When the prefrontal cortex isn't wired properly it effects one's ability to process information correctly, it makes a person more apt to rely on *emotion* rather than *fact* to make decisions. Remember that "Tea Party" test? Ask your liberal friend or family member that question, their response should open your eyes, and the miswired prefrontal cortex, well, that becomes a LOT more convincing. Their ability (inability) to support their *beliefs* with facts, will be enlightening.

If you're a conservative, and you've ever had a discussion on topics such as we've discussed in this book with a liberal, you probably witnessed something interesting. The liberal is likely to become *agitated*, to say the least, perhaps ending the conversation abruptly with some expletives; such is the nature of *emotion vs. fact*. The casual liberal often doesn't want to discuss politics with a conservative, they probably know, or would quickly find out, that they rely on *emotional* arguments, and don't have facts to back up their flimsy philosophy. The liberal is likely to 'unfriend' the conservative in their online world. The conservative is more likely to try to *discuss* differing opinions.

When a rally or protest occurs, which is most likely going to involve violence? A Tea Party protest, or a Black Lives Matter protest? Who is likely to DO the violence at a Trump rally, Trump supporters or Trump haters? In general, who is more prone to violence, liberals or conservatives? If we use liberal vs. conservative demonstrations and protests, the answer is clear, it is liberals who most often turn to violence. Liberals tend toward shouting people down, shutting up dissent, shutting down free speech, not allowing the Conservative speaker on the college campus, closing down businesses, *forcing* people to bow to their beliefs, and violence. *Emotion vs. fact.*

Ok, this turned out to be a bit more of a manifesto than I had originally planned, but in the end, I've done what I wanted to do. For we conservatives, I have tried to set some things straight, and maybe your liberal friends or family will 'get you' a little better if they read this, *but probably not.*

For you liberals, I hope I opened your eyes a bit, to what the media has done to you. *(I'm guessing few if any liberals actually sat though this tongue-lashing.)* You liberals bit the hook and they reeled you in, you became a parrot repeating lies and distortions, and maybe *now* you see a little clearer, but, *I doubt it.*

The End

To my daughters, I hope you took the time to read this, 'really' read this, it was short for a reason, you shouldn't be able to say you didn't have time to read it. And, I'd expect a letter from you, telling me how wrong I am about all this, and using some convincing arguments. I'd expect that, but, the convincing argument part, I doubt it. I imagine the argument will center on emotion rather than fact, maybe you'll prove me wrong. And, sadly, I doubt that my daughters even read this book, they probably stopped after reading the title.

A parent can't mold a child in their image, not usually, and I tried to encourage my kids to think for themselves, and they have, sort of. But they've bit the hook, the liberal media, liberal peer group, liberal professor hook. But there's something to remember, I said it earlier:

~

We need to start with the premise that sometimes someone is wrong, and someone is right, and sometimes it's just a matter of personal preference, not necessarily right or wrong.

*But, and this is important, sometimes, yes, sometimes, someone IS **right**, and someone IS **wrong**. That's important to remember! Especially if YOU are wrong.*

Epilogue

And, the truth of the matter; conservatives and liberals tend to preach to their prospective choirs, and preaching to the *other* choir, well, they won't change their tune, just as we conservatives can't suddenly understand the distorted emotion-based rhetoric of the liberal. And a book like this… get out your hymn book.

A little recap: *(Generalizations that are generally true)*

• Conservatives don't care about people's skin color. Liberals are OBSESSED with skin color.

• Conservatives think much of the LGBTQ movement is not *normal*, and are opposed to normalizing such aberrant behavior, but, most of us are kind and respectful to people, regardless of their beliefs. Conservatives see the danger in transforming society into some gender neutral nirvana, because gender differences are profound, and bathroom/locker room/shower restrictions are there for a reason. The LGBTQ movement seeks to blur the differences between genders, and to put into *law* those blurred lines, which conservatives see as obvious dangers.

• Conservatives see the "Man-made Global Warming" agenda as a tool for massive government control and manipulation of our entire economy, and realize that cutting back energy sources means massive price increases for power, which will slow down and harm our economy. Liberals would dial back our economy, do away with coal and 'fossil fuels' and allow some United Nations panel to dictate just how much we can or can't expand our economy.

• Conservatives hate women. *(I was going to say 'don't' but I think this statement is ridiculous enough to leave as is. If you believe this, well, like I said, liberals have some brain issues.)*

And, I was going to 're-cap' more of what we've talked about but, I won't. I've sung to my choir, and you liberals, well I have no idea what you think of all this, except that most likely you believe the title of the book was appropriate.

P.S.

One last thing.

From time to time I'll get into some back and forth with a liberal, "friend." You can't win, since the liberal, if confronted with irrefutable proof that their view is incorrect, will proceed to stick to their *preferred*, <u>incorrect</u> view. I actually had a liberal, after hearing such irrefutable proof that they were wrong, tell me that they "Prefer their version." Logic, and the truth, will not win the day with liberals, they'll simply dismiss it. (Pre-frontal cortex)

One thing I figured out, and will probably present at the outset the next time I'm faced with some debate with a liberal, is to remind them of this; and I'll probably read this statement, to save some time:

"If you didn't frequently, strongly, and repeatedly, criticize Barack Obama, and you had eight years to do it, then I don't care what you think about the current President. You have lost any credibility with me. You are obviously blinded by some misguided party or liberal loyalty. You are a liberal lemming marching in line, a parrot who simply repeats what you've been fed by your liberal media, without any attempt at critical thinking. Go away."

I think that's reasonable.

Lance Hodge

"If you find yourself *shouting* the truth, you may actually be drowning it out."

"When those on *your side* act like an angry mob, you might have picked the wrong side."

Other books by Lance Hodge:

The Poison of Political Correctness, By Lance Hodge
ISBN-10: 1514166488   ISBN-13: 978-1514166482

The Common Sense Guide to: DEALING WITH THE POLICE
By Lance Hodge
ISBN-10: 1514339579   ISBN-13: 978-1514339572

Epiphany: *The Student's Guide to thinking RIGHT*
By Lance Hodge
ISBN-13: 978-1519714145

Available at:

AMAZON.com, Booksamillion.com,

Barnes & Noble, and other fine booksellers.